21st Century Skills Library

GLOBAL PRODUCTS

BICYCLES

Robert Green

Cherry Lake Publishing
Ann Arbor, Michigan

Published in the United States of America by Cherry Lake Publishing
Ann Arbor, MI
www.cherrylakepublishing.com

Content Adviser: Scotford Lawrence, Curator and Historian, The Cycle Museum

Photo Credits: Cover and page 1, © Michael DeYoung/Corbis; pages 5 and 6, © Bettmann/Corbis; page 12, © Wolfgang Rattay/Reuters/Corbis; page 14, © Grand Tour/Corbis; page 17, © Tibor Bognar/Corbis; page 18, © Michael S. Yamashita/Corbis; page 22, © Bojan Brecelj/Corbis; page 23, © Anthony Redpath/Corbis

Library of Congress Cataloging-in-Publication Data
Green, Robert, 1969–
  Bicycles / by Robert Green.
    p. cm. — (Global products)
  ISBN-13: 978-1-60279-024-7 (hardcover)
  ISBN-10: 1-60279-024-8 (hardcover)
  1. Bicycle industry—Juvenile literature. I. Title. II. Series.
  HD9993.B542.G74 2008
  338.4'76292272—dc22   2007003883

*Cherry Lake Publishing would like to acknowledge the work of
The Partnership for 21st Century Skills.
Please visit* www.21stcenturyskills.org *for more information.*

TABLE OF CONTENTS

CHAPTER ONE

THE PERFECT VEHICLE

Asger Knudsen pulled his bicycle off the school bike rack and breathed a weary sigh. He had just had a grueling after-school soccer match. His knees were scraped, and he had missed his chance for a goal. His team had lost, and the last thing he wanted to do was to pedal for the next hour to get home.

Asger, like so many Danes, had been riding a bike for as long as he could remember. He pulled up the collar on his coat and pedaled off under overcast skies. Denmark, a **Scandinavian** country just to the north of Germany, has long encouraged the use of bicycles as a form of cheap transportation. Bicycles also don't release the smoggy exhaust of an automobile.

The bicycle is something of a famous symbol in Scandinavia. It has a special place in the history of the area. During World War II, Denmark's Prince Frederick and his wife, Ingrid, rode bicycles around Copenhagen, the capital city, to show their support for common people during difficult times. Their fellow European monarchs, Queen Juliana and her daughter Queen Beatrix of the Netherlands, were also known for riding bicycles. As a result, the royal families in these countries are sometimes known as the "bicycle monarchies."

The first bicycles had no pedals or gears.

The first bicycles were invented in Paris, the capital of France, in 1817.

A German named Karl von Drais devised a machine that had two wheels

and was mounted like a bicycle, allowing people to get around with much

less effort. He called it the *laufmachine*, German for "running machine."

The laufmachine looked just like a bicycle, but it lacked the gears and

pedals that make a modern bicycle so easy to ride. Unlike the rider of a modern bicycle, the rider of Drais's invention pushed off the ground and cruised

Riding Karl von Drais's bicycle was like walking with wheels.

for a distance. It was a bit like walking with wheels, and the fun part was always going downhill, when no pushing was needed at all.

Inventors searched for an even easier way to harness the power of a rider's legs. They eventually added a chain that connected the revolving pedals to the back wheel. Thus the modern bicycle was born, and people, just like Asger and many other Danes, have been pedaling ever since.

Asger was reluctant to pedal home, but imagine how he would have felt if he'd had to walk. The bicycle, one of the simplest forms of transportation, allows people to travel farther and faster. The practical appeal of the bicycle caused it to spread quickly around the world, and today, bicycles are found in every corner of the globe.

It might be hard to imagine now, but women once had a hard time moving around freely. They were discouraged from venturing out alone, and they had few of the legal protections they enjoy today.

In the 19th century, a group of women known as suffragists worked together to obtain greater legal rights for women—especially the right to vote. These women hailed the bicycle as "the freedom machine," since it gave them an easy way to get around. The new freedom allowed them to be more independent and have more control over their own lives. This is just one of the social impacts of the invention of the bicycle.

CHAPTER TWO

THE HEART OF THE BICYCLE

Melted iron is poured in a foundry, a place where metal ores are made into metals and metal alloys.

As Asger pedaled away on his modern, titanium, 10-speed bike, he began to hear thunder rumbling in the distance. "Great. Just what I need!" he thought. He had only been riding for 15 minutes, so he still had another 45 minutes to go. "At this pace," he thought, "I'll arrive home drenched!" He began pedaling a little faster, trying to hurry home and beat the oncoming storm.

The bicycle is a relatively simple machine, but it has become more complex over the years. The reason is the application of new technologies to the manufacturing process. The frame of a bicycle, for example, would appear to be the simplest part of all, since it has no moving parts. It is the bicycle's central component, and other parts—like the wheels, handlebars, and seat—are attached to it.

The earliest bicycle frames were made of wood and later of steel. Wooden bicycles, however, were prone to breaking. Using steel made the frame less likely to break, but heavier. Bicycle makers tried to find new ways to make the bicycle light and strong—the two principle qualities of a good frame. To get these qualities, bicycle manufacturers turned to the science of **metallurgy**—the study of metals. Metal comes from ores found in the earth. Scientists can isolate the metals from ore to make metal objects. These objects are shaped by heating them in furnaces. Metals can also be combined with other metals and nonmetals to make **alloys** that are lighter and stronger.

Manufacturing a bicycle frame has become a highly scientific process, and bicycle manufacturers have become quite skilled at making metal alloys for frames. Columbus Tubing in Milan, Italy, is one company that has been working to make better frames since 1919. The company specializes in making tubing, hollow metal rods that are formed into diamond-shaped bicycle frames.

Raw materials arrive at the Columbus factory, with labels describing the purity and composition of the metals. The factory then combines the metals into various types of tubing, such as aluminum and steel alloys.

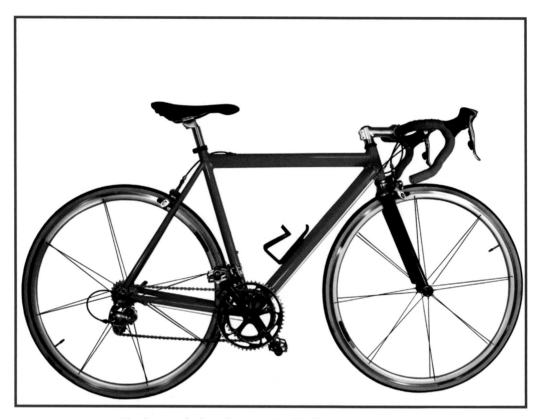

The frame of a bicycle is made of hollow metal rods. Can you see the diamond shape in this bicycle frame?

Today, products are often not made by just one company or in just one place. Columbus Tubing makes only the tubing for bicycle frames in their metalworking factory. These frames are then purchased by bicycle makers all over the world and used to make the final product. The wheels, handlebars, seats, gears, and other parts are made by different companies.

Bicycles and bicycle parts are made by companies located around the world.

Learning & Innovation Skills

What is a good job for someone who loves bicycles? One answer would be engineering.

Imagine yourself as an engineer who designs faster bicycles. How would you try to make bicycles faster? What do you think racing bicycles will look like 25 years from now?

CHAPTER THREE

A PASSION FOR SPEED

As if things couldn't get any worse for our young biker, small raindrops began to fall onto the streets of Denmark. Asger, trying desperately to get home before the weather got any worse, kept his mind off the rain by imagining he was the great Lance Armstrong, the famous seven-time Tour de France winner, racing to the finish line.

Lance Armstrong crosses the finish line at the 2004 Tour de France.

Italy is another country in which many people have a passion for bicycles. Since the early 20th century, Italians and other Europeans have used bicycles as a cheap form of transportation. But many Italians also have a love of racing bicycles. This has inspired bicycle makers all over Italy to turn their skills to the creation of fast-moving bikes.

The most famous race in Italy, the Giro d'Italia, was begun in 1909. It is a major international event, and along with the Tour de France and Spain's Vuelta a España, it is one of the three grand tours of bike racing.

Today, races are big business. Managers organize them, corporate sponsors feature their logos on tracks and on riders' jerseys, and professional sporting organizations oversee the whole show. Just imagine how many careers one can pursue in bicycle racing alone.

The complex business of racing has sparked a fierce struggle to make the lightest, fastest bikes.

21st Century Content

The business of sports extends beyond the making of sporting products, such as the bicycle. The Giro d'Italia, for example, was started to boost the circulation of La Gazzetta dello Sport, an Italian newspaper. The newspaper sold more copies by featuring stories about the race they helped to organize.

Bicycle makers often sponsor riders and share the triumph of victory when their creations carry riders across the finish line ahead of the others.

Because racing bicycles take more effort and attention to produce, and because they are much more expensive, fewer are made. As a result, the industry has something of an old-fashioned, family atmosphere.

Spectators cheer on the bicycle racers at the Giro d'Italia.

This is true, for example, of the bicycle factory belonging to Irio Tommasini, once an amateur racer. As a young man, Tommasini couldn't stay away from bicycles, and when he wasn't racing, he worked in a bicycle factory in Milan. There he learned about the care that went into making a racing bicycle.

Competitive by nature, he set up his own bicycle company in 1957 in his hometown of Grosseto, in the Tuscany region of Italy. Tommasini bicycles today are among the most famous in the world, and the factories use highly scientific means to constantly improve the bikes' speed and performance.

Tommasini crafts its own frames by hand and adds a particularly fine finish. Where does the factory in Grosseto get the tubing for these frames? Columbus Tubing in Milan is one supplier. Tubes from the Milan factory are loaded onto trucks and driven to Grosseto. There the tubes are crafted into Tommasini frames, to which pedals, forks, and other parts are added.

Tommasini only makes between 2,000 and 2,500 bicycles a year, most of which are **exported** to other countries for sale. A distribution and sales network connects the factory with the **markets** where people want to buy the bicycles. Traveling on trucks across land and by ship across the ocean, Tommasini bicycles are then sold by **importers** as far away as Japan and Australia. These importers work with the bike company, often communicating via the Internet to place orders and arrange for shipping.

At the very end of this long line—from metalworking specialists to **distributors**—is a customer, who can ride with dreams of winning the Giro d'Italia.

Racing bikes are just one kind of bicycle manufactured today.

CHAPTER FOUR

CROSSING BORDERS

Even though Asger isn't always thrilled about riding his bike from one place to the next, he isn't the only one who uses this great mode of transportation. Many people all over the world, from America to India and even Japan, use bicycles as their only mode of transportation. Bikes are better for the environment and great for exercise, and you don't have to pay for car insurance!

People around the world use bicycles for transportation. These children in Cambodia are riding their bikes home from school.

A worker welds bicycle parts in a factory in China.

None of those reasons mattered to Asger now, though. The rain started falling heavily, and the thunder was getting louder and closer. He pedaled as fast as he had ever pedaled, in spite of being tired from his soccer match. He was only 10 minutes away from home! Would he beat the worst of the storm?

Although bicycle manufacturing began in Europe, the majority of bicycles are now made in India and China. This pattern reflects the trend in global manufacturing. So many products today are made in the East that countries such as China have become the world's leaders in manufacturing.

What is it that India and China offer modern manufacturing that other countries don't? The answer is found in their large populations and their stage of economic development. China has the world's largest population, and India the second largest. They are the only two countries in the world whose total populations number more than one billion each. These populations are eager to work and willing to work for modest pay. This means that China and India offer a source of inexpensive **labor** to manufacturers. And because of the inexpensive labor, manufacturers can keep the prices of products down and sell their goods more cheaply.

The move of bicycle manufacturing from West to East—from Europe and the United States to India and China—reflects this search for inexpensive labor. But something very interesting happened along the way. The **technology**, or know-how, to make bicycles was transferred to the same countries used as a source of labor. This happened in two ways.

In India, the British introduced the bicycle while India was a British **colony**. The cheap form of transportation proved so appealing to the large Indian population that Indian companies soon began making bicycles to sell in the local market.

Kaohsiung is the second-largest city in Taiwan.

In China, the story needs the introduction of a third actor. Taiwan, an island off the coast of China that was separated from the mainland after a civil war, began making bicycles at the request of foreign companies. Those companies sought a source of inexpensive labor at a time when China was closed to foreign companies. The Taiwanese quickly learned the methods of making bicycles and then started to make them under their own brand names.

This represented a step up the production ladder—the second part of the answer to what India and China offer modern manufacturing. The most valuable part of producing a bicycle is not the manufacturing, but the value added by selling the bicycle under a well-known brand name. So when Taiwanese companies began to sell bicycles under their own names, they made more money.

As the Taiwanese made more money, however, their workers became more expensive. Labor costs, in other words, rose. Manufacturers in Taiwan turned to a giant source of inexpensive labor—mainland China—just across a narrow waterway known as the Taiwan Strait. The Chinese speak the same language as the Taiwanese and share the same cultural heritage. This made for a natural relationship between the two.

Today, many Taiwanese companies produce goods mainly in China. The Taiwanese company

Giant both produces and sells bicycles in different countries. This makes it a **transnational** company—a company that crosses borders in its business. Today, it is often difficult to clearly define a company by nationality. Giant, for instance, is a Taiwanese company, but many of its employees are Chinese and European. In fact, even the executives in Taiwan are sometimes not from Taiwan at all. Business is increasingly less tied to a single location or a single nation.

This means that people who work for transnational companies must be able to communicate with people from different cultures. They must be open to new perspectives and be able to collaborate with people from many different backgrounds.

Giant is one of the largest bicycle manufacturers in the world. Giant began by making bicycles for Western companies, which were sold under the brand names of the companies that placed the orders. But to improve profits, Giant eventually began selling bikes under the Giant name.

Giant manufactures and assembles bicycles in China and in Taiwan. Most recently, Giant opened a bicycle factory in Europe, to sell to the market there. And so the production story comes full circle—West moves East, which heads back to the West.

Workers polish and assemble bicycles in a
Giant bicycle factory in Taiwan.

CHAPTER FIVE

PEDALING ON A GLOBAL PRODUCT

Many families ride bicycles for fun and fitness.

At first glance, global bicycle manufacturing appears to be split between West and East. In Europe and the United States, bicycle makers produce expensive, high-end bikes, often for racing. In the East, manufacturers make less-expensive bicycles for everyday use. This is true up to a point, but the industry is evolving.

Mountain bikes are good for rough terrain.

As the Taiwanese and Chinese mastered the skills of bicycle making, they also began to experiment with manufacturing their own bicycles. Companies like Giant now also create top-of-the-line bicycles. Companies in the West make less-expensive models for everyday bicycle riders like Asger Knudsen in addition to high-end bikes.

The important point is that the technology washes back and forth like waves in the sea. An innovation by one bicycle maker inspires the others to create new bicycles. This process results in ever-better bicycles. This is known as technology transfer, and the result is a truly global bicycle industry.

Many manufacturers continue to specialize in certain parts. Some companies, such as Columbus, make tubing for the frame, while others make rubber for the tires or advanced gear mechanisms. Many manufacturing processes have become so complicated that companies use

Some manufacturers specialize in making gear mechanisms.

Some companies specialize in making bicycle seats.

computers and advanced machinery to help guide their production and achieve a level of precision not possible by humans alone.

This **specialization** has resulted in a supply chain that involves the entire globe. Parts flow in and out of different countries. Bicycle makers make some parts and buy others, combining them in their assembly plants.

Inexpensive labor continues to play a part in global manufacturing. Factories are still most likely to be located in places with lots of people who will work for lower wages. But the complexity of bicycle making today requires a high level of technical knowledge that can be found all over the world.

At the end of this global production chain are the buyers of new bicycles. Those buyers, spread as widely around the globe as the makers, choose the bicycles that suit them best—a mountain bike, a racing bike, or just a simple bike to get them home from school.

∾

Lightning began to crash in the skies directly above, just as Asger pulled his bike into his garage. His mom was inside, ready to collect his wet jacket, shoes, and socks.

"That was fast!" she exclaimed, amazed by how quickly Asger got home. "It took you 47 minutes, a new record. Imagine how wet you would have been if you didn't have a bike!"

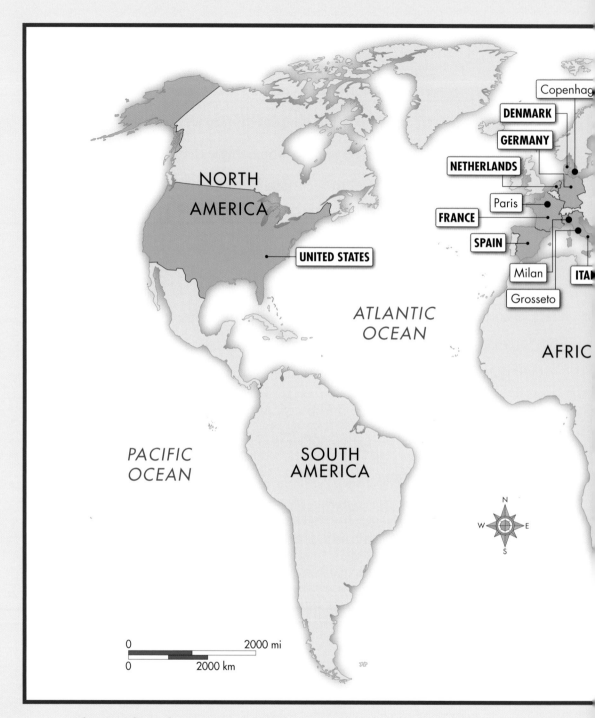

This map shows the countries and cities mentioned in the text. They are the

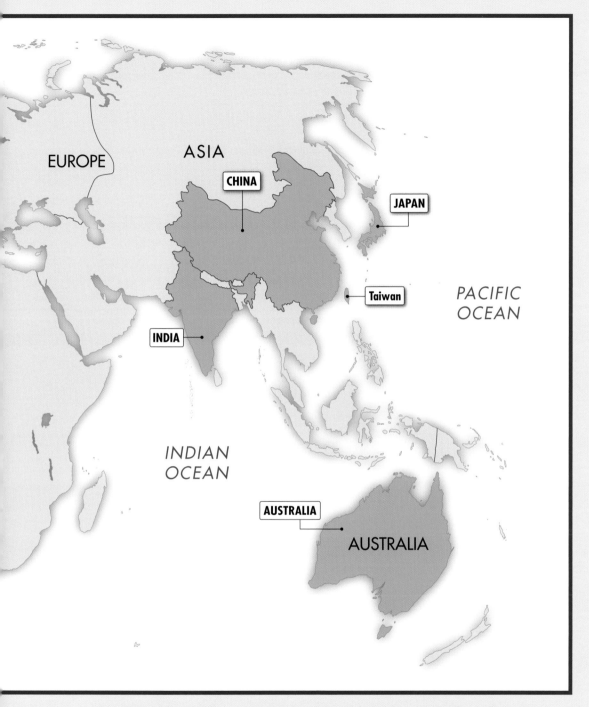

locations of some of the companies involved in the making and selling of bicycles.

Glossary

alloys (aa-LOYZ) metal products made by combining different metals with nonmetals

colony (KOL-uh-nee) a place or group of people ruled by a foreign government

distributors (dis-TRIB-yoo-turz) people or companies that get products from where they are manufactured to places where they will be sold

exported (ek-SPORT-ed) sent (as in products) to another country to be sold there

importers (im-PORT-erz) people or companies that bring foreign goods into a country to be sold

labor (LAY-bur) a group of workers who work for wages

markets (MAR-kits) places where goods or services are sold

metallurgy (MEH-tuh-lur-gee) the science of metals and their uses

patent (PAT-uhnt) the legal document giving an inventor the sole rights to manufacture and sell his or her invention

Scandinavian (skan-di-NAY-vee-uhn) of or having to do with the region of northern Europe made up of Denmark, Norway, and Sweden

specialization (spesh-uh-lih-ZAY-shun) the act of focusing on a particular part of a process

technology (tek-NOL-uh-jee) the application of science and engineering to the process of making products

transnational (trans-NAH-shun-uhl) something that goes beyond the borders of one nation

FOR MORE INFORMATION

Books

Buckley, Annie. *Be a Better Biker.* Mankato, MN: The Child's World, 2006.

Haduch, Bill. *Go Fly a Bike! The Ultimate Book of Bicycle Fun, Freedom, and Science.* New York: Dutton Children's Books, 2004.

Teichmann, Iris. *Globalization.* North Mankato, MN: Smart Apple Media, 2003.

Web Sites

How Things Work: Bicycles
howthingswork.virginia.edu/bicycles.html
To learn more about the science of bicycles

Pedaling History Bicycle Museum: A Quick History of Bicycles
www.pedalinghistory.com/PHhistory.html
For more information on the history of bicycles

INDEX

ABOUT THE AUTHOR

Robert Green is the author of three other books in this series—*MP3 Players, Cars,* and *Skateboards*—and many other books for young adults. He holds graduate degrees from New York University and Harvard. He learned a great deal about globalization while living in Taiwan, where he studied Chinese and worked for the Taiwanese government.